Original title:
Meaning: A Riddle No One's Solved

Copyright © 2025 Creative Arts Management OÜ
All rights reserved.

Author: Clara Whitfield
ISBN HARDBACK: 978-1-80566-270-9
ISBN PAPERBACK: 978-1-80566-565-6

## Whispers of Enigma

In a room full of clocks, time stands still,
The cat on the shelf is plotting a thrill.
A shoe on a desk, what could it mean?
Perhaps it was worn by a fish in a dream?

A chicken in boots walks across the floor,
Clucking out riddles, always wanting more.
With feathers all ruffled, it hides in plain sight,
It chuckles and dances, delighting the night.

## The Unfolding Puzzle

A hat made of soup, how odd it may sound,
Spoons scattered wildly, they dance all around.
An elephant juggling with jellybean chairs,
What's next in this circus? Who really cares?

A pickle plays chess with a lonely ol' gnome,
They argue in silence but never feel home.
Winning or losing, it's all just a game,
In this quirky world, it's all rather tame.

## Secrets in Shadows

In shadows, the laughter is curious, bright,
A robot with dreams takes a fly in mid-flight.
With circuits that tickle and wires that hum,
It whispers to cats and invites them to drum.

A broom that can dance, but only at noon,
Swings with a mop, under the light of the moon.
They twist and they twirl, as if leading a fight,
Stirring up giggles, oh what a delight!

## **Fragments of Understanding**

A hat made of cheese hides thoughts so profound,
With snickers and giggles as answers abound.
A walrus in sneakers plays hopscotch alone,
Chasing the echoes of a mystical tone.

A sock and a spoon share a secret so deep,
Together in dreams where the absurd takes a leap.
They dance through the twilight, avoiding the light,
In a world of confusion, where nonsense feels right.

## **The Code of Life's Tapestry**

In the loom where yarns collide,
A sock took off on a wild ride.
It chased a shirt with stripes so bright,
In our wardrobe's soft moonlight.

The pants grew legs and started to dance,
While belts just sat, lost in a trance.
But every garment had its say,
Spinning tales both bright and gray.

## Secrets Woven in Dreams

In dreamland where the pajamas play,
A fluffy cloud became a sleigh.
With pillows steering through the night,
They giggled past the stars so bright.

A teddy bear tried to take the wheel,
But snores erupted like a meal.
They crashed into a cake, oh dear!
With frosting smiles, they showed no fear.

## Laughter in the Afterthought

A thought strolled in with mismatched shoes,
It tripped and fell, gave us the blues.
But then it laughed, got up to dance,
Wiggling around in sheer romance.

The echoes of its clumsy feat,
Left everyone laughing in their seat.
A message sent from silly minds,
Said life's too short for ties that bind.

## The Veil of Understanding


Behind the curtain of our minds,
A squirrel's plan is hard to find.
It gathers nuts, tells clever jokes,
While thinking deep like great old folks.

We ponder what the nuts could mean,
While squirrels chuckle, feeling keen.
Maybe life's just one big game,
Where acorns roll and laughter reigns.

## Overture to the Unanswerable

A cat in a hat sings on the floor,
While socks on the ceiling debate what's in store.
If fish could dance, would they fly in the air?
Or would they just flounder, not really care?

The toaster speaks wisdom, but only in toast,
And waffles hold secrets they like to boast.
Is life's biggest question, just what's for lunch?
Or is it the number of sprinkles in a crunch?

A giraffe plays chess with a frog on a bike,
Each move met with laughter, they both just like.
If laughter's the answer, then what's the delight?
Is asking for answers just chasing the light?

When donuts wear bow ties, and coffee gives cheer,
Is that when we feel that the joke's crystal clear?
As riddles jiggle while giggling along,
We find out the punchline is just where we belong.

## Veins of Intuition

A penguin in slippers struts down the street,
He claims he's the king of the high-flying fleet.
If dreams come with toppings, do clouds yell for spritz?
Or are they just puffy and playing with wits?

A squirrel with glasses reads books upside down,
While goldfish debate who wears the best crown.
If wisdom's a noodle, is pasta the sage?
Or just slippery noodles that dance off the page?

Why do we ponder the fluff in our heads?
While the plants in the garden converse with the dreads.
If rocks could take selfies, would they smile and pose?
Or would they just ponder the size of their toes?

An ant plays the banjo; his bandmates are flies,
They bring down the house with their musical sighs.
In this playful world, where oddities bloom,
We search for the questions beyond all the gloom.

## Delicate Threads of Doubt

A snail sings a tune with a rhythm quite slow,
While butterflies giggle at places they go.
If clocks were to dance, would they twist or would spin?
And would they still count all the seconds within?

A cactus in slippers dreams of the rain,
While daisies juggle and murmur in vain.
Are shadows born secrets that sunlight will tell?
Or just tiny stories, saying all is well?

Why do ants wear boots on a quest to the moon?
Do pretzels feel twisted, or just need a tune?
If a sandwich could talk, would it say, "I'm great,"
Or would it just wonder what's up on its plate?

In puzzles and riddles, we teeter and dance,
Chasing odd echoes, we dare them to prance.
With humor as tether, let laughter abound,
In this tangled web, hilarity's found.

## **The Landscape of Inquisition**

A raccoon in a helmet conducts the parade,
With marshmallows marching, all dressed for charade.
If jellybeans whispered the tales of their fight,
Would candy say "Nope, we prefer chunky light?"

A llama debates with a wise old tomcat,
On what brand of nonsense has title to that.
If bubbles are thoughts that escape from our lips,
They float with delusion on hilarious trips.

Why do clouds argue the shape of a shoe?
And why do we giggle when skies turn to blue?
If laughter's the answer, let's say it's a game,
Turning life's riddles into a playful fame.

In this quirky world, where questions are spun,
We chase after giggles like rays from the sun.
With whimsy and wit, our adventures unfold,
In the riddle of life, let the laughter be bold.

## Whispered Secrets of the Soul

In the corner, shadows dance,
Lost in thoughts, caught in trance.
What's the key to unlock the door?
Giggling whispers, can't take it anymore.

The cat knows, with a knowing stare,
Pondering why we bother to care.
Chasing questions, round and round,
Finding answers upside down.

A puzzle box with no clear face,
Playing hide and seek with grace.
What's the joke? Who crafted the jest?
A ticklish thought, let's take a rest.

In the garden of whimsical quest,
Silly ideas grow, they're the best.
Peeking through the windows wide,
What's inside? A silly ride!

# The Echo Chamber of Inquiry

A question bounces off the wall,
"Why do we trip, why do we fall?"
Echoes giggle back with glee,
"Maybe it's just meant to be!"

A mirror asks with a cheeky grin,
"Tell me, where does all this begin?"
The ceiling laughs, "You're such a brain,
Can't you see it's all in vain?"

With every riddle that we weave,
The answers hide, oh, what a tease!
Tickling thoughts in various tones,
Whispers drift like silly drones.

In the chamber filled with quirk and jest,
Curiosity wears a funny vest.
Seeking truths in shadows cast,
Are we just running from the past?

## The Tapestry of Unknowing

Threads of chaos, woven tight,
Each color blends, a strange delight.
What's the meaning? Who can tell?
Perhaps it's best to ring a bell.

In patterns spun of yarn and fluff,
We search for wisdom, but it's tough.
Tangles knot, and laughter flows,
Should we unravel? Who knows?

Every loop is a giggling sigh,
What's the truth? Let's give it a try!
With every stitch a question grows,
A tapestry that jests and glows.

Dancing threads in playful spree,
A fabric of absurdity!
We wrap ourselves in joyful hues,
Searching for the light-hearted clues.

**Stories that Time Forgot**

Old tales whisper, 'Where'd we go?'
A game of tag with time, you know?
Memory dances, a jester's play,
Tickling fancies, come what may.

Forgotten legends, bold and bright,
Turn mundane days into delight.
What's a story without some cheer?
A punchline missed? Oh dear, oh dear!

Like shoes misplaced in a funny race,
We chase the tales with goofy grace.
Every twist, a laugh or frown,
Who needs a crown when you wear a gown?

Dusty pages turn with flair,
Spinning yarns floating in the air.
Timeless giggles linger on,
Where are we now? Oops, they're gone!

## Keys Lost in the Mist

In pockets deep, they hide away,
Those keys that jingle, then stray.
A puzzle wrapped in fabric lost,
Searching high, and what a cost!

Behind the couch or under the bed,
Where do all these lost things tread?
With laughter mixed in every hunt,
We joke about the crazy stunt.

A laundry basket plays the trick,
While clocks and mugs raise havoc quick.
The hunt is on, no end in sight,
Chasing items through the night!

But when they're found, it's quite absurd,
"Right where I left them!" we'd all heard.
In echoes of the past we trust,
Who needs the keys? Oh, what a bust!

## The Unwritten Parable

Once upon an untold tale,
A chicken crossed, its fate set sail.
But why, we ask, it made that leap,
And silence fell, a secret deep.

A duck rolls eyes; it quacks, confused,
"Just for the fun, or simply amused?"
The rooster crows with grand disdain,
"Is it wisdom, or just plain pain?"

Curiosity, it takes its toll,
For every question starts to roll.
Instead of answers, we have more,
The stories drift like leaves ashore.

In laughter, lessons come undone,
Finding truth can be such fun.
With every twist, a giggle yields,
Unwritten tales fill all the fields!

## Whispers of the Unknown

There's a ghost in my cereal bowl,
It tickles my spoon, what a role!
With giggles and sighs in morning light,
I ponder if it's joking outright.

The milk says, "Splash," the toast just grins,
While crumbs jump and perform their sins.
Is breakfast a stage for wild charades?
Each breather laughs as silence fades.

In shadows stretch, the pancakes sway,
Do they dance while I'm far away?
A mime in the kitchen, who needs that?
When sweet syrup tells a tale that's flat.

So here I sit, my bowl in hand,
Deciphering breakfast's quirky band.
In every crunch, a riddle spins,
The unknown giggles, and so it begins!

# **The Dance of Doubt and Certainty**

In the ballroom of the mind's delight,
Doubt leads first, in heels so bright.
With twists and turns, it sways so swift,
While Certainty, it just plays the drift.

They tango hard with steps unsure,
In every shuffle, we want a cure.
But laughter echoes on the floor,
As thoughts collide and hopes explore.

A waltz of wonder, a two-step bust,
Doubt likes to tease, while Certainty must.
They bump and jiggle, what a sight,
With silly grins, they're both polite.

As the music fades, they bow their heads,
Together woven like tangled threads.
In their quirky dance, we find a cheer,
For life's odd rhythm is perfect here!

## The Specter of Clarity

In the corner, truth wears a hat,
It conjures smiles, then scatters like a cat.
Questions float like balloons in the air,
Each pop a chuckle, oh, isn't life fair?

Clarity winks with a mischievous grin,
It dances in circles, where do we begin?
With every answer, a new question sings,
Life's a puzzle made of rubber bands and strings.

## Waves in the Sea of Ambiguity

Surfing on questions with googly eyes,
Each wave a riddle, oh what a surprise!
The ocean of thoughts stirs with a laugh,
A fish of confusion swims in my path.

I ride the crests of uncertainty's throne,
Splashing my thoughts, like they're made of foam.
Every toss of the tide brings dizzy delight,
While seagulls squawk questions all day and night.

# The Paradox of Certainty

In a world of truth that swings like a door,
Certainty giggles, saying, 'But wait, there's more!'
It taps my shoulder, then runs out of sight,
Leaving me puzzled, oh what a fright!

Like socks in the dryer, facts spin around,
One moment they're here, the next they're not found.
Certainty's a jester in a fool's parade,
Laughing as logic plays tricks in the shade.

**Traces of the Unveil**

Behind the curtain, shadows do flit,
They tease with whispering giggles that fit.
Each trace of truth wears a silly disguise,
Peeking through laughter with bright, twinkling eyes.

The unveil promises peek-a-boo fun,
Where every answer's just another pun.
In this circus of thought, we all play a part,
Chasing our questions like kids in a cart.

## **Kaleidoscope of Questions**

Why does a banana never feel blue?
It peels back layers, just like a clue.
In a world full of giggles and grins,
The jester's the sage where the laughter begins.

What's green and sings? Elvis Parsley, they say!
It spins round and round in a comical play.
Chasing the thoughts like a cat with a mouse,
The riddle's the fun in this zany house.

## The Search for Clarity

Was that a sneeze or a guffaw?
Confusion reigns, oh what a flaw!
A fortune cookie teased on my fate,
Only told me to eat, don't wait!

The cat with the hat is missing a shoe,
Should I worry or join in the brew?
Peering through fog with a spoon in my hand,
Clarity dances, a whimsical band.

## Gaps in the Narrative

Once there was a knight who fought with a spoon,
Searching for stories that vanished too soon.
With a dragon of doubt in a castle of cheese,
He hoped for some wisdom, or maybe a sneeze.

The jester sat silent, the bard broke a string,
In the gaps of the narrative, laughter can sing.
What's lost in the gaps is just part of the tale,
As we sail with the whimsy, we'll never turn pale.

## **Signals from the Uncertain**

When life gives you signals, just dance in the rain,
With rubber ducks floating, and laughs as your bane.
A signpost that winks, what could it mean?
Perhaps it's just here to steal the scene!

The squirrels were plotting in question marks,
With nuts for their wisdom, they eavesdrop like sharks.
In the echoes of laughter, we puzzle and play,
For signals from whimsy can brighten the day.

## **Beyond the Veil of Knowledge**

In a room full of books, I thought I was wise,
But the cat on my lap seemed far more surprised.
She purred with delight at the chaos around,
While I scratched my head, looking lost and unbound.

With puzzles and equations, I stared at the page,
My thoughts all jumbled, like a monkey in a cage.
"Just love the banana," she softly insisted,
As I furrowed my brow, some truths had been missed.

The cosmos revealed, or did it just tease?
Like an itch in your ear that nobody sees.
In laughter we find, perhaps just a laugh,
Might hold the key to our colorful path.

So here I sit wondering, with questions galore,
As the cat rolls her eyes and starts to snore.
Beyond all our pondering, what seems so profound,
May just be a cat nap that's profound underground.

## The Chasing of Answers

I went on a hunt for some solid advice,
But the goldfish just gawked, and looked rather nice.
With a shrug and a flip, it made quite the scene,
As I chased all the bubbles, like some kind of queen.

Questions, they danced on a tightrope of thought,
Teetering between what I had and I sought.
In a circus of logic, I lost my last clue,
The jester was laughing, he knew what I knew!

With a twist and a turn, my brain did a flip,
That yellow balloon was my ultimate trip.
For while I was busy, the answer found flight,
It waved from the clouds on a glittery night.

So I laugh at my quest, oh the joy of the chase,
When the answers are hidden, they dance without grace.
Perhaps it's the chase that brings giggles and grins,
As we travel through riddles, our folly begins.

## Shadows of What We Seek

In shadows we wander, looking for clues,
While a squirrel overhead laughs at our blues.
He nibbles on acorns, totally unfazed,
At the humans confused, in a whimsical daze.

The ghosts of our questions look quite bemused,
As we scramble like kids, all gloriously bruised.
With a wink and a nod, they vanish like smoke,
Leaving us giggling, while we think, "How bespoke!"

Through corridors twisty, we tiptoe and peek,
Are we following shadows or just feeling weak?
Between giggles and riddles, we dance through the haze,
As laughter unravels the most puzzling maze.

So let's raise our teacups, to shadows that play,
To questions that tumble, and whisk us away.
For in this silly search, we find what we seek,
Might just be the laughter that makes our hearts leap.

## Ephemeral Clarity

A bright light shone down, then it flickered and flared,
Like thoughts in my head that were blissfully bared.
In a carnival ride, my brain starts to spin,
With clarity teasing, but not letting me in.

Just when I decided to grasp at the thought,
It danced 'round my vision, as if it were caught.
I chased 'round the merry-go-round of my doubt,
While giggles erupted, and grew into shouts.

In the depths of confusion, a bubble did rise,
With smiles and laughter, like stars in the skies.
I realized that grasping was not what I craved,
But the joy of the journey, the wild ride I braved.

So here's to the moments that shimmer and shine,
That tickle the funny bone, all yours and all mine.
In ephemeral clarity, we lose and we find,
The best of our riddles are wrapped in good times.

## Trails of the Elusive Answer

In the woods of thought we play,
Chasing clues that skitter away.
A squirrel giggles, hides its snacks,
While we ponder on the tracks.

Around the tree, the whispers groan,
Is it a riddle or a clever drone?
We follow footprints made of jokes,
Dancing shadows, giggling folks.

A turtle claims he's got the key,
But he's too slow, just like me.
The answer sings in silly rhymes,
Yet we're lost in tangled chimes.

So grab your maps of silly shapes,
We'll search for truth like little apes.
With each mishap, we'll share a laugh,
Life's questions turn to silly path.

## The Alchemy of Thought

Stir the pot with dreams and schemes,
Mixing giggles, laughter beams.
What's the secret? Who can say?
Alchemy has its funny way!

A wizard in a floppy hat,
Turns his wand into a cat.
The potion bubbles, colors clash,
Suddenly—POOF! It's gone in a flash!

Each thought a sprinkle in the air,
Bouncing round without a care.
Can nonsense shape the world anew?
A magical conundrum, who knew?

Take a sip of silly soup,
Join the wild and wacky loop.
In this brew, we laugh and shout,
Finding answers we're all about.

## Reflections of the Unseen

In a mirror where questions collide,
The answer plays a funny ride.
What is truth? What is fair?
Oh look! A monkey in my hair!

Behind a fog, the jester's grin,
Dances like it's made of spin.
We search for pearls, find only shells,
Riddles hiding behind the bells.

Jump through puddles of snickering prose,
Who needs wisdom in silly clothes?
The glass reveals a jester's dance,
With every turn, a new mischance.

Full of quirks, our thoughts will sway,
In the mirror, they run away.
Giggles echo in the unseen,
Reflecting riddles, pure and keen.

## Pathways Through the Fog

Wander through this moody mist,
With every turn, you'll laugh, you'll twist.
Hidden paths with giggles glow,
Up ahead, a squirrel steals the show!

Laughter bubbles in dreamy haze,
Each step reveals a wacky maze.
What's that sound? A bubble burst?
Oh look, it's just a bubble first!

No clarity when whimsy reigns,
But joy is found amidst the chains.
We skip along the squishy ground,
In unseen riddles, laughs abound.

So grab your hat, let's dance in fog,
Embrace the silly like a dog.
For in this playful, funny land,
The answer's just a joke, unplanned!

## The Horizon of Wonder

Why does the sun take its time to rise?
The stars giggle, in endless disguise.
Clouds play hide and seek with the light,
While birds chirp secrets of day and night.

What's the color of a thought in the air?
A rainbow giggles, without a care.
Wind whispers riddles we haven't heard,
As leaves dance softly, no clue inferred.

Is laughter the answer to every quest?
Even the worst of jokes can jest.
A tickle, a giggle, a grin, a sigh,
The horizon beckons, oh my, oh my!

So chase the clouds, and ride the breeze,
In this world of wonders, do as you please.
For questions abound, like stars in the sky,
The horizon of wonder, oh my, oh my!

## Conundrum Beneath a Surface

What's swimming below in the watery deep?
A fish in a bowler hat? Or dreams that leap?
With bubbles like giggles escaping the sea,
The surface conceals what's puzzling to me.

A turtle is thinking, what's five times a snail?
His world is a puzzle, a curious tale.
As jellyfish wobble, and seahorses dance,
The ocean teases, it laughs at chance.

Mermaids are grinning, as sailors will shout,
Awaiting the answers they're all about.
Each wave brings a riddle, and then some more,
Unraveled questions, washed up on the shore.

So dive in with wonder, let currents lead,
In the conundrum's embrace, see how it feeds.
For beneath every surface, a joy we shall find,
A world full of giggles, so cleverly designed.

## The Garden of Unspoken Thoughts

What blooms in the garden of things left unsaid?
A daisy of silence? Or a tulip in red?
With whispers of wishes tucked under the dirt,
And secrets that giggle, but never assert.

Here shadows are chatting, in shades of green,
Gnome friends are debating the sights they've seen.
The roses are winking, the daisies are shy,
While the wind carries laughter, drifting on by.

Elves plant new riddles amid leafy dreams,
Where chatter of tomatoes is bursting at seams.
And pondering parsnips talk day and night,
A comedy garden, what a delightful sight!

So wander this haven, take time to explore,
For thoughts unspoken can open a door.
In this garden of wonder, let laughter take root,
As every small giggle dances in pursuit.

## Chasing the Faint Glow

What's that shimmer just out of reach?
A firefly's giggle or a glowing peach?
In the dark of the night, what beckons your eye?
A riddle of light that flutters on by.

Is that the moon winking with mischief and fun?
While shadows are laughing, they've only begun.
With footsteps of whispers, they're tiptoeing near,
The glow's just a tease, it vanishes, dear.

What's hidden behind the curtain of night?
A dance of delight, a faint little light?
Chase it and stumble, then laugh when you fall,
For the glow you're pursuing is teasing us all.

So follow the flicker, through laughter and cheer,
For riddles and giggles are always quite near.
The faint glow is dancing, whimsical, bright,
In the chase, there's no answer—just pure delight!

## The Allure of Ambiguity

In the land of mixed-up signs,
Where answers hide behind the blinds.
A chicken dances, a cat sings tunes,
What's the truth? Who knows, just cartoons!

Contradictions play in a park so bright,
They flip and flop, oh what a sight!
A squirrel speaks, yet none can hear,
Mysteries tickle, they bring us cheer!

So let's embrace this silly game,
With puzzles and riddles, none the same.
Laugh out loud, share a wink or two,
In this chaos, joy finds its cue!

The joy of questions, a riddle's delight,
In the fog of nonsense, we find our light.
So ask away, with a chuckle or shout,
For in this madness, we figure it out!

## In Search of Hidden Keys

With keys that jingle but doors that vanish,
I search for answers, but they all banish.
A signpost points, but it makes no sense,
A riddle disguised in a vague pretense!

The map I follow is upside-down,
A penguin leads me while wearing a crown.
Each twist and turn, a laugh or a scream,
I'm lost in a world that's not what it seems!

Where did they hide those puzzling clues?
In a toaster? A sock? Or under some shoes?
We giggle and jolt with each failure we greet,
Searching for wisdom in a web of deceit!

But in this search, love blooms all around,
For laughter and joy in confusion are found.
So onward we trot, with glee in our hearts,
In this game of life, we each play our parts!

# A Tapestry of Intrigue

In a tapestry woven with laughter and tears,
Lies a riddle of life that spans all the years.
A cat in a hat plays games of charades,
While a wise old owl swoops down and parades.

The threads of confusion weave patterns of fun,
Like a dance in the moonlight, or a race from the sun.
Each stitch holds a story, a quirk or a jest,
What's the meaning? We're all just guests!

A twist here, a loop there, the fabric goes wild,
Reality giggles, it's like being a child.
Embrace every knot, for it ties us together,
In this whirling dervish of life, light as a feather!

Let's unravel the humor in this crazy art,
For wisdom is hidden, but joy's in the heart.
The more we untangle, the more we can play,
In this wild tapestry, let laughter have sway!

## Journey through the Unknown

Pack your bags, it's time to roam,
Through a land where nonsense feels like home.
A cactus sings a quirky song,
In a world where nothing's really wrong.

Flip a coin to choose your path,
Heads means laughs, tails means math!
With each strange turn, we giggle and spin,
In a chase for the riddles we can't wait to win!

A map of giggles, a compass of fun,
In this journey, we laugh, we run!
Through forests of whimsy, over streams of joy,
Each adventure a treasure, nothing to cloy!

So let's celebrate the odd and bizarre,
In the unknown, we'll find our star.
With laughter our guide, we'll wander with glee,
For in this wild journey, we find you and me!

## The Labyrinth of Insight

In a maze where thoughts collide,
A chicken crossed and tried to hide.
Was it looking for a clue?
Or just waiting for a shoe?

Round the corner, wisdom lurks,
With a smirk and funny quirks.
What's the point? The signposts joke,
"Follow me, I'm just a bloke!"

Pondering in the twisty paths,
Searching hard for clever laughs.
Every turn, a silly sign,
"Lost? Just sip this funky wine!"

In the end, we laugh and play,
The wit turns night into the day.
So wander in this playful storm,
And keep your quirky mind warm!

**Ripples in the Stream of Thought**

In waters deep where thoughts are tossed,
My brain's a boat that's always lost.
Paddle hard, but here I float,
Chasing bubbles, what a joke!

Each ripple's laugh, a fleeting guide,
With fish that dance and ducks that slide.
Catch a thought, but it will flee,
Swim behind, you'll not catch me!

Waves of wisdom crash and play,
While silliness rules the day.
"Splash me once, you'll bloom anew!"
And so I splash, right back at you!

In this stream of jumbled glee,
The meaning's lost, quite merrily.
So dive right in, no need to pout,
The fun's in swirling all about!

# The Language of the Unsaid

In silence thick, where whispers dance,
Words waddle by, missing their chance.
What's unsaid? A wild charade,
Like socks on dogs in a parade!

Chirps and grunts in odd delight,
Make meanings twist and take to flight.
The cat's meow speaks volumes clear,
But still, I scratch my head in fear!

Gesture wildly, wave a hand,
Play charades, a riddling band.
What's the vibe? A secret code—
Lost in translation on this road!

So here we are, a riddle's cue,
No dictionary will pull you through.
In laughter's glow, we'll find our say,
While meanings frolic far away!

## Fragments of the Indiscernible

In a puzzle made with silly pieces,
Where logic stops and laughter increases.
What is here, a part or whole?
It's like a donut out of control!

Each fragment holds a quirky truth,
Like gum on shoes or spilled vermouth.
Mix it right, a cocktail of glee,
But fill the glass with total spree!

Jigsaw minds in mismatched styles,
Comically lost in kiddie miles.
Fit me there, or is it wrong?
The pieces twirl and sing a song!

So here we stand, a puzzled crew,
With laughter's light to pull us through.
In pieces we may never find,
Yet in the fun, we've crossed some lines!

## The Unraveling Thread

In a world where socks go to hide,
One wonders where they take their ride.
Button lines that never fit,
And rules that say, lie just a bit.

What's left after the punchline's told,
Is it courage, or just being bold?
A yarn so tangled, lost to time,
We'll knit our thoughts, one line at a rhyme.

The cat's out, but the mouse is shy,
Both stare at the cheese with a glint in the eye.
So what's the joke? Is it understood?
Or just another scratch in the wood?

Stitch by stitch we pull at this thread,
Laughing at things we all nearly dread.
And in the end, is it all just fluff?
Or is it wisdom wrapped soft enough?

## Masks of Perception

Wear a grin, it's all a charade,
Behind the comedy, who's truly afraid?
Jesters dance under a moon made of cheese,
While wise men chuckle, hoping they please.

Peel away layers, what do you find?
A wiggly worm or a sharp-witted mind?
In clown shoes, we stumble, tripping for fun,
But maybe the punchline is never quite done.

A wink from a joker, a jest from a queen,
In a circus of life, can laughter be seen?
With masks in our hands, we play a charade,
Is the truth in our laughs or merely betrayed?

As shadows blend, we chuckle at fate,
For laughter's a riddle we never quite rate.
Behind every mask, a heart finds its space,
In the comedy club, we all find our grace.

## **Windows to the Unattainable**

Through panes of glass, we squint and gaze,
At colorful dreams lost in a haze.
Frogs in tuxedos leap without fear,
While bicycles fly, and dogs stop to cheer.

A window swings open, a breeze gives a shout,
What lies beyond is what life's about.
So we peer through the glass, with curiosity rife,
Will we spot the punchline in this riddle of life?

Cats chase their tails – oh what a sight!
While birds play chess 'til they take flight.
The world spins by with a giggle of time,
As we turn the key to this riddle in rhyme.

Perhaps the answer is just out of reach,
Like fish in a tree, or a dog learning speech.
But in every window, a chuckle remains,
To lighten our hearts and untwist our chains.

## The Silent Query

A question looms, as cats gather round,
Whiskers twitching, without a sound.
What's the secret behind that door?
A biscuit or adventure? Who knows for sure?

The goldfish swims in circles of thought,
While the parrot squawks what the human forgot.
In the silence of pondering, giggles take flight,
As the punchline waits, just out of sight.

Oh, the mystery wrapped in a silly disguise,
Like why socks vanish, to everyone's surprise.
Rhymes twist and turn, like a playful dive,
Keeping us guessing, feeling alive.

So ponder the queries that tickle your brain,
In the land of the wacky, we laugh through the pain.
With questions so fluffy, they bounce like a ball,
The truth's just a jest, in the end after all.

## Searching for Significance

Where's the treasure? I ask in jest,
Is it hidden beneath this worn-out vest?
I find socks and crumbs, but no gold,
Maybe life's mysteries are just tales retold.

The cat stares back, she's in on the game,
Dare I say it's all pretty lame?
Is the secret in pizza or donuts to munch?
Alas, all I find is an empty brunch.

## In the Silence of Questions

Why do cows jump over the moon?
Do they chase stars while humming a tune?
I ponder and ponder, coffee in hand,
But the answers are stranger than I had planned.

Is the sky just a giant blue kite?
Or the universe playing hide-and-seek tonight?
Questions boil over, like soup gone wrong,
But hey, that just means I can sing my song.

## Parables of the Enigma

A penguin waltzes on an icy floor,
Meanwhile, a llama sings folklore.
What's the lesson in this strange parade?
Maybe it's dance, or some ice cream raid?

The wise owl hoots, 'It's all a big joke!'
Before I realize, I'm just a bad bloke.
Keep searching for gems, buried in jest,
Perhaps they taste sweeter when laughed at best.

## The Horizon of Uncertainty

At the edge of the world, I squint and stare,
Is that a mirage, or a floating chair?
My buddy insists it's a UFO sighting,
But honestly, it looks more like cloud writing.

Chasing horizons, we find more grey,
Is it confusion, or just a lazy day?
Either way, a chuckle comes easier than dread,
Maybe solace lies in the things left unsaid.

## Mysteries Beneath the Surface

In a pond where the frogs wear hats,
Bubbles rise, they speak in spats.
Why does the goldfish glow so bright?
Is he just showing off tonight?

A turtle spinning tales quite tall,
Claims he once raced with a beach ball.
But who really knows what's the truth?
It's all quite silly, so uncouth.

A duck quacks rhyme, it's true, they say,
But no one quite knows what's at play.
Chasing shadows, they wear their frown,
Yet giggles echo all around.

So let's dance with the quirks we find,
Each laugh entwined with the crazy mind.
As the world spins round, we play this game,
Where one silly thought is never the same.

## Conundrum of Shadows

In a world where the shadows are blue,
They whisper secrets to me and you.
A cat with a monocle, quite profound,
Reveals life's puzzles through giggles unbound.

A lamp post chats with the nightingale,
"How do I swim in this curious gale?"
"Oh hush!" says the moon with a cheeky grin,
"It's all just a dance, let the fun begin!"

The clock ticks slowly, or maybe it's fast,
Time laughs at puzzles that never quite last.
Images jiggle, dissolve in the air,
Can a riddle be found, anywhere, anywhere?

So gather round for this merry spree,
Let's tickle our brains until we agree.
With silliness floated like dandelion seeds,
The shadows just chuckle, fulfilling our needs.

## **Veiled Truths in Twilight**

In twilight's grasp, truths dance like stars,
Wearing funny ties, and silly scars.
A rabbit juggles carrots and dreams,
While laughing at life's oddball themes.

The trees stand tall, but one's quite round,
He claims he grows roots underground.
While whispers of wishes flutter in the breeze,
A butterfly giggles, "Don't take it with ease!"

With clouds that chat about yesterday's snack,
And suns that play hopscotch on the track.
What's hidden in humor, one might inquire?
Could it be folly, or just pure desire?

Join in the revel, let's turn up the fun,
With riddles and giggles, we're never done.
As the veil of twilight looms large, it seems,
Life is but laughter wrapped in our dreams.

## The Dance of Paradoxes

A fish on a skateboard, what's the fuss?
Says he's got tricks, like hopping a bus.
But wait! There's a dog who claims he can fly,
With bubbles and giggles that float to the sky.

The cactus in clogs joins the groove,
Says, "Dance with your prickles, just feel the move!"
A parrot squawks riddles, all twisted and bright,
"Are you the dancer, or lost in the night?"

A maze of confusion wrapped in delight,
What's wrong and what's right? Who's losing their sight?

The answers dissolve like ice in the sun,
In a world spun with laughter, we all come undone.

So twirl in the paradox, leap like a cat,
Join the shenanigans, let's go tit for tat.
Life's just a puzzle that's made to bemuse,
As we dance through the chaos, let's spread the good news!

## Mysteries in the Heartbeat

Why does my heart race for cake,
But slow down for the time I fake?
Jellybeans dance in my chest,
Are they the answer? Just a jest!

Bouncing thoughts like a bouncy ball,
Do they mean I'm having a ball?
Or is it just caffeine's sweet thrill,
Giving my heart quite the spill?

Whispers of love or the pizza I crave,
Are they the secrets that hearts misbehave?
With every thump, a silly delight,
Solving this riddle, it just feels so right!

So I giggle at pulses and beats,
Who knew a heart could dance in such feats?
In the end, it's a laugh we embrace,
Life's little quirks, a joyful chase!

## Portals to the Unimagined

Jumping through portals, oh what a sight,
Where socks pair up and dance in the night.
Imagined worlds, where pineapples sing,
Throw in a giraffe, now that's my fling!

Underneath beds, where monsters convene,
They sip on tea, and discuss what we mean.
A donut with wings flies over a cat,
In this oddball realm, where chaos is at!

Chasing rainbows that giggle and snort,
On jellybean clouds, we all cavort.
In lands where the secrets pink elephants hide,
And laughter is currency, come take a ride!

So let's toast to mysteries, funny and grand,
In realms where the ridiculous takes a stand.
With joy in our hearts, let's leap and play,
For life's greatest puzzles are silly today!

## Collage of the Inexplicable

A canvas unraveled, with colors so wild,
Bananas in pajamas, like a mischievous child.
Unicorns prancing on marshmallow beams,
Reality's bursting at the seams!

Why is my sandwich a jigsaw of cheese?
Is the pickle laughing? It's such a tease!
In corners where silence holds a loud snort,
Here's a riddle that retorts what we thought.

Magic is just when the fridge starts to hum,
As cakes wear sombreros, oh, here they come!
The absurd is a puzzle crafted with flair,
With each silly stroke, we giggle and stare!

In this gallery of whimsy and fun,
Let's paint over logic, let laughter run!
For every odd riddle we long to embrace,
In life's playful mess, we find our place!

## Shadows of Existence

In shadows that dance, a peekaboo fright,
Do they then giggle when I turn on the light?
With peeks and whispers, they tease and they jest,
Could they reveal what's truly expressed?

Noses of pumpkins wearing top hats,
Invite me to join their bizarre chats.
What quips shall I hear in the dark of the night?
Are these shades figments, or just my delight?

Crouching low, they tell tales absurd,
Like fish that fly, or a word unheard.
What nonsense they peddle, oh what a scene,
In shadows of laughter, where I've never been.

So here's to the echoes, both silly and bright,
In the gallery of shadows, our quirks take flight.
Unraveling laughter in every disguise,
The jests of existence, in hilarity lies!

## The Puzzle of Existence

Why does toast land butter-side down?
And why do clowns wear that silly frown?
The universe spins, a topsy-turvy dance,
As we chase our tails in a bewildered trance.

What's the deal with socks that never match?
And why do we call it a 'fishing' scratch?
Life hands out riddles like a carnival prize,
Squirting silly questions right into our eyes.

Do fish ever get thirsty, you think?
Or is that just another puzzling wink?
We laugh at the quirks, we giggle and grin,
While the answers hide where the jokes begin.

In this grand game, we all play our part,
With riddles and rhymes that tickle the heart.
So join in the fun and don't look too hard,
The answers are hidden in the backyard!

## Enigmas in the Silence

Why do we park in driveways so tight?
And why do we sleep with our heads at night?
The clocks tick and tock, with no reason to show,
As silence wraps tightly, a riddle in tow.

Is that a duck, or maybe a cow?
Or is it just nonsense, like here and now?
The whispers of questions float up to the sky,
Like balloons filled with laughter that just pass us by.

Can a sandwich really be a part of our day?
Or is it just bread on some silly cliché?
With giggles and chuckles, the puzzles arise,
From the depths of our fancies, where nonsense defies.

In the quiet of thought, with a wink and a grin,
The riddles of life lead us back to begin.
So question the silence with flair and with cheer,
For the funniest answers are often unclear!

## Clues Hidden in Time

Why does time tick by when you're having fun?
Yet drags like a snail when the work has begun?
Each second a puzzle, like ducks in a row,
As moments collect in a grand overflow.

If two's a company, then what's one's a crowd?
And how can you whisper while singing out loud?
With laughter and doubts wrapped tight in a rhyme,
Oh, the clues of existence dance sweet in our time.

If clocks can run backwards, then what's time but play?
A mischievous jester, who leads us astray.
With each tick that passes, each giggle we hear,
Life's riddles unfold as we steer clear of fear.

So gather your musings, your thoughts like balloon,
And float them like feathers beneath the bright moon.
For in every riddle lives joy in disguise,
A treasure chest waiting in life's funny lies!

# Unanswered Questions Beneath Stars

Why do stars twinkle while we sit in awe?
And how does the moon have a pull like a law?
In the cosmos we ponder, with spirits so bright,
As questions spin wildly in the cool, dark night.

Can you really count all the grains of the sand?
Or is that just a riddle too grand for the hand?
We gaze at the heavens, each star a delight,
While scratching our heads in the soft, starry light.

Is it true that the grass is greener next door?
Or are we just stuck with what's hard to ignore?
With laughter like stardust, we chase down the clues,
Of the giggles and whispers that life often brews.

So raise up your eyes to the sparkling display,
And let your curiosity lead you away.
In the universe's jest, we find fun and cheer,
As unanswered questions draw us ever near!

## Patterns in the Chaos

In a world where socks take flight,
The cat sits plotting all the night.
Jellybeans dance on the kitchen floor,
While I wonder what life has in store.

The boxes pile up, quite a sight,
Full of things that just feel right.
Yet, where's that left shoe I once admired?
It's vanished like dreams that never expired.

Puzzles with pieces all curved and round,
Ask the fridge why it makes that sound.
Perhaps it's a code the dog can decode,
While I sit here, with my snacks, feeling old.

So find the fun in the disarray,
Laugh at the mess and the bits that stray.
For in this chaos, a pattern you'll find,
Maybe it's just life trying to unwind.

## The Threadbare Journey

Worn-out shoes take a stroll, it seems,
Through fields of fluff and sunset beams.
Sailing on clouds of sticky glue,
They wonder where all the socks flew.

Underneath a candy-cane sky,
A pickle flew past, oh my oh my!
The compass spins, it lost its way,
As jellyfish blooms in the ocean's ballet.

With a map that's just a doodle of fun,
They search for gold where the hoot owls run.
But every step seems to lead them back,
To the same old tree with a laughing snack.

So grab your backpack, pack it tight,
For this ride's about to take flight.
Fall in love with the absurd and bizarre,
As we chase our tales, near and far!

## Constellations of Quandary

Stars halted in a funky dance,
Look closely, you might catch a glance.
A flying spaghetti monster ascends,
To tie together where logic bends.

Question marks float on candy clouds,
While elephants dance, oh they're so proud.
And puzzles sing their silly tunes,
While the moon sneezes, with all its swoons.

Galaxies swirl in a giggling spree,
As bananas argue over tea.
Where did that comet go, dear friend?
Maybe it's lost, trying to pretend.

So gaze at the sky, have a good laugh,
At this cosmic riddle, a wacky path.
For in the stars, with their winks and grins,
Lies a universe where nonsense wins!

## Lighthouses in the Gloom

In foggy nights, the flickers beam,
Chasing shadows, a playful theme.
Seagulls argue, with a laugh and squawk,
While the lighthouse winks, a quirky clock.

Old ships dance like rusty tunes,
In a serenade beneath the moons.
While fishes gossip in a bubble bath,
Counting stars while drawing a math.

With candles thrown in the stormy sea,
And crabs that think they can rhyme with me.
Navigating troubles as though a game,
In this watery world with no shame.

So let the light guide your way through the dark,
For there's laughter hidden in every spark.
In the gloom where the silliness roams,
May we find our way, wherever home.

## Mirages in the Mind

In a desert of thoughts, I chase a mirage,
With a glass of lemonade, and a mischievous barrage.
I ponder my socks, where did one go?
It danced with the breeze, said 'Hello!' to the fo' sho'.

The cat's got the answers, or so I believe,
When I asked for wisdom, she just took a leave.
I tickle her whiskers, she yawns with delight,
As if the secrets of life hide way out of sight.

Why do ducks quack, and why do geese honk?
Do they know the treasures in a house made of junk?
I see a parade of mismatched socks here,
It's a festival of fun, come join, don't you fear!

As I wander this maze of the mind's crazy dance,
I trip over riddles that leave me askance.
But laughter's the answer, or so it's been said,
With a smile on my face, onward I tread.

## The Ocean of Ambiguities

Diving deep in a wave of mixed-up clues,
I find a school of fish wearing bright shoes.
They giggle and splash with a shake of their fins,
In a sea of confusion, where humor begins.

A crab wears a crown, while a turtle plays drums,
Underwater disco, oh, how the fun hums!
Jellyfish spark joy, a glow in their dance,
But can they tell secrets? Not even by chance!

A lighthouse stands empty, with bulbs all aglow,
It points out direction, yet nowhere to go.
Each wave whispers riddles, but none are to hear,
Just the laughter of waves, that brings us good cheer.

In this ocean of nonsense, let's float for a while,
With a boat made of laughter, let's drift and let's smile.
For in waters so murky, the joy springs out wide,
In the tide of absurd, we shall merrily ride.

## Footprints on the Canvas

A canvas so blank, like a fresh slice of bread,
First comes a paw print, then a hotdog instead.
With colors of ketchup and mustard, I see,
A masterpiece forming, just wait, let it be!

The paint splatters laughter, it giggles and spins,
Like a rollercoaster ride where everyone wins.
A duck in a top hat, a pig doing ballet,
Who knew art could giggle and lead us astray?

Footprints of joy, while cats bring some sass,
They prance on the colors, oh, what a mishmash!
With every odd splatter, I ponder and muse,
Is this art or a party where nonsense peruse?

In a gallery filled with glitter and glee,
I dance with each paint stroke, oh so carefree!
For the canvas tells stories, all funny and bright,
In the footprint saga, I find pure delight.

## The Portrait of Unriddled Life

A portrait hangs crooked, with a smirk on its face,
It winks at my questions, and takes off in a race.
With colors that clash and a nose out of place,
It tells me to laugh, it's afraid of the chase.

A dog wears a tux, and a cat's in a gown,
They dance through the canvas, a royal renown.
With each little twirl, and a curtsy so sweet,
They sweep through the room on their very own feet.

Chasing the answers, I trip on a shoe,
That once belonged to a kangaroo crew.
They tiptoe around, with a grin so fishy,
In the portrait of life, where absurd is all squishy.

The brush strokes giggle as they swirl and they play,
Each hue's an adventure, come join in the fray!
For in this grand portrait, where laughter ignites,
We find joy in the chaos of beautiful sights.

## Threads of Intrigue

In a web of yarn, I fight with a cat,
Socks disappear, where's my favorite hat?
Twisted plots in the laundry await,
Did the washer elope? I just can't relate!

A penguin was dancing, or so I was told,
In a world full of socks, I'm feeling quite bold.
My toast speaks in riddles, the butter won't spread,
Is breakfast just chaos? I'm dreading my bread!

Noodles and sprinkles, together they jump,
A unicorn's dress code? It's all just a thump.
A pickle's great wisdom is lost in the jar,
Yet here I'm just panicking, stuck in my car!

Puppies and puzzles, they're all in a race,
Chasing their tails, but can't find their place.
If jelly beans chirp, I might just give in,
To join this mad circus where chaos can win!

## The Silent Symphony of Thought

In my head, a concert of thoughts takes the stage,
A quacking duck solo, should I turn the page?
Cotton candy clouds drift, tickling my mind,
Where's that elusive rhyme? I'm left in a bind!

The squirrels hold meetings, plays in the trees,
Plotting world domination, or maybe just cheese.
A banana in shades tells secrets to peas,
While spaghetti serenades the buzzing of bees!

Do dreams come with snacks, or is that just me?
A dance-off of shadows beneath a tall tree.
Cartwheeling cups whisper, "Have you seen my shoe?"
Can laughter be bottled? Let's make it, just two!

Melodies linger like ice cream in June,
While teacups are plotting beneath the bright moon.
Tickles and giggles weave threads into sound,
In this silent tomfoolery, joy can be found!

## Whispers of the Unexplained

A cat on a skateboard, the ultimate dare,
It voyages through kitchens, causing despair.
The toast pops up laughing, I think it's a prank,
Toaster conspiracies, or so people think!

Chickens in tutus parade down the lane,
Contemplating life, are they really insane?
Why do socks vanish? The dryer may know,
A clandestine party, where lost items go!

In the garden, the gnomes discuss a tall tale,
Of flying goldfish and a pie without scale.
Where's my missing left shoe? I'd love to investigate,
Yet simply I giggle, it's all up to fate!

Turtles in sunglasses, they glide with such ease,
Spreading the news like a soft summer breeze.
The whispers grow louder, and soon I will hear,
What secrets do vegetables hide in their cheer?

## Shadows in Untold Stories

A shadow in corner whispers tales in the light,
Of spaceships flying past, in the blink of a night.
What do they drink at their cosmic café?
Is pizza still pizza, in a dance far away?

Clouds wear their hats, spiffy and bright,
While beans bloom like flowers, taking their flight.
The laughter of spoons as they twirl through the air,
What rioting objects? Is life really fair?

Invisible unicorns prance through the parks,
Kicking up giggles, leaving colorful sparks.
A pancake philosopher ponders life's truths,
As syrupy wisdom drips down to our youths!

In these hidden shadows, the silliness reigns,
With cacti that dance and go wild with their gains.
A whimsical mystery, tangled and bright,
In these playful places, all seems just right!

## Echoes of Forgotten Truths

In the land where wisdom hides,
A goldfish speaks of tides.
Yet the cat in glasses sighs,
While the dog just plods and tries.

Chasing shadows of the past,
Hoping knowledge comes at last.
But the answers play hooky,
Leaving us all feeling kooky.

Pondering in the sunny noon,
Where does the missing sock go soon?
A missing link from yesterday,
Like sunshine on a cloudy day.

With laughter ringing in the air,
We search for truths that disappear.
In a world so filled with jest,
We giggle through the little mess.

## The Quest for What Lies Beyond

On a quest for hidden clues,
A squirrel wore bright pink shoes.
Chasing thoughts that spin and dance,
Finding answers by mere chance.

On a hill, we boldly stand,
Searching with a stick in hand.
But the clouds just laugh and tease,
As we stumble through the trees.

The sun sets down in splashed hues,
While the owls share their news.
To find what lies beyond the veil,
Just follow that silly snail trail.

So, let's tiptoe through the night,
With a feather, maybe it'll bite!
For what we seek, we can't explain,
Lives inside a rubber chicken's brain.

## **Faces in the Abyss**

In a mirror dark and deep,
Winked a face that made me leap.
Silly grins and wobbly frowns,
Playing kings and wearing crowns.

The abyss, it chuckles loud,
With shadows hiding in the crowd.
Every glance a twisty tale,
Like bubbled tea that's gone stale.

I chase my thoughts, they run in pairs,
While a sock sings and a shoe declares.
What shapes lurk within the dim?
A parade of nonsense, full of whim.

Yet in this pool of giggling fright,
The truth hides just out of sight.
So let's dance with faces weird,
As we toast with cups of beard.

## The Links of Conundrum

In a chain of puzzling links,
A penguin winks and drinks.
Flap your wings, say it loud,
Confusion's wearing a clown's shroud.

Knots tied in a mental dance,
The weasel giggles at the chance.
Each question pulled a different thread,
While the goldfish dreams of bread.

A loop-de-loop in thought we ride,
With questions hanging like a tide.
But laughter echoes with each twist,
What's the answer? Oh, what a mist!

So we laugh till our sides are sore,
Searching for clues forevermore.
In this game where nothing's clear,
Let's toast to riddles we hold dear!

## The Lure of the Unspoken

In whispers soft, secrets hide,
Like socks lost in the laundry tide.
Questions dance, a curious spree,
What's the punchline? Not a clue, just glee.

A frog in a suit, where's the joke?
Maybe he's learning, or just a bloke.
The plot thickens, yet bends and sways,
While laughter echoes through the maze.

A cat with a hat, ponders the sun,
Is life a game? Or just for fun?
We puzzle on, with hats askew,
In life's grand play, what can we do?

The silence speaks, yet tickles the mind,
In riddles wrapped, the truth we find.
So let's toast to questions, big and small,
With goofy grins, we'll solve them all!

## Hints of the Unfathomable

A pickle walks into a bar, don't ask why,
It chuckles and beams, feeling spry.
What's the purpose? Who knows for sure,
As giggles float like a sweet perfume.

A fish in glasses, pondering deep,
Why jump to conclusions, when you can leap?
In shadows roam, mysteries glide,
Is the joke on you, or just on the ride?

With rubber chickens dancing in tune,
They ponder life under the goofy moon.
What's the score? Not a game in sight,
Just playful quirks and laughter's delight.

So here's to questions, bold and bright,
To chase the absurd, with sheer delight.
We tickle the mind, in whimsical spree,
To catch the uncatchable, just let it be!

## When Wonder Takes Flight

A snail in sneakers, on a grand run,
Off to find riddles, just for fun.
What's the rush? The world spins slow,
But in his heart, oh, how dreams glow!

A chicken in woods, pondering space,
Does the egg have a goal? A comical chase!
Laughter erupts amidst leafy quests,
The answers are winks, playful tests.

A hamster sketches the stars with flair,
Drawing up puzzles, floating in air.
Each twinkle a riddle, a wink, a giggle,
In the heart of the unknown, mysteries wiggle.

So pack up your joy, and don't be shy,
For wonder awaits, oh my oh my!
Chase the unknown with a smile so bright,
For life's little secrets are pure delight!

## The Refrains of Mystery

A banana wearing shades, strolling with flair,
Sings to the stars, do they even care?
Questions bounce like jellybeans, light,
In a world where answers always take flight.

A sock puppet knight, guards fluffy quests,
In search of the truths that life jest.
What is reality? A slippery slope,
But let's ride the tide, we'll find our hope!

A disco ball ghost, dancing with glee,
Of life's odd puzzles, we're all so free.
With humor in hand, and a heart so kind,
We'll festoon the night, in laughter entwined.

So join in the fun, in a world so bright,
Where questions are laughs under moonlight.
With each silly riddle, we float and sway,
In the wacky great mystery, we play and play!

www.ingramcontent.com/pod-product-compliance
Lightning Source LLC
Chambersburg PA
CBHW071843160426
43209CB00003B/391